RSVP
RAINTREE
STECK-VAUGHN
PUBLISHERS
A Steck-Vaughn Company
Austin, Texas
www.steck-vaughn.com

A LOOK AT LIFE IN

The **Nineties**

Judith Condon

Published by Raintree Steck-Vaughn Publishers,
an imprint of Steck-Vaughn Company

Printed in Italy. Bound in the United States.
1 2 3 4 5 6 7 8 9 0 04 03 02 01 00

Library of Congress Cataloging-in-Publication Data
Condon, Judith.
The nineties / Judith Condon.
        p.   cm.—(A look at life)
    Includes bibliographical references and index.
    Summary: Traces the events, trends, and
    important people of the 1990s, including science,
    technology, fashion, music, art, architecture,
    sports, entertainment, and news.
    ISBN 0-7398-1341-2
    1. Civilization, Modern, --1950—Juvenile literature.
    2. Nineteen nineties—Juvenile literature.
    [1. Nineteen nineties. 2. United States—History—
    1969. 3. United States—Social life and customs—
    1971-]
    I. Title. II. Series.
    CB429.C66 2000
    909.82'9—dc21   99-37295

Cover photographs

Top left: Nelson Mandela, April 1990
(Topham Picturepoint)

Top right: Dolly the Sheep, February
25, 1997 (Popperfoto)

Center: Ricky Martin became a major
success in the late 90s
(© AP/Wide World Photos)

Bottom left: The Spice Girls at the
1996 Smash Hits Poll Winners Party
(Topham Picturepoint)

Bottom right: Rollerblading (Pam
Francis, Robert Harding Picture
Library)

Acknowledgments
The Author and Publishers thank the following
for their permission to reproduce photographs:
Camera Press: pages 4-5b, 6b, 7t, 18t, 18b, 19b,
20t, 21l, 24b, 27t, 36b, 37b, 38t, 41; Popperfoto:
pages 4t, 5t, 6t, 7b, 8, 9t, 9b, 10t, 10b, 11t, 11b,
12, 14t, 14b, 15, 16t, 17, 19t, 20b, 21r, 22t,
22b, 23t, 23b, 24t, 25t, 25b, 26, 27b, 28, 29t,
29b, 30, 31t, 31b, 32t, 32b, 33, 34t, 34b, 35, 36-
37t, 38b, 40t, 40b; Robert Harding Picture
Library: pages 16b (NASA/Phototake NYC), 39
(Pam Francis); Science Photo Library: pages 13t,
13b; AP/Wide World Photo: 19t, 31b.

Quotations are from: page 4: Nelson Mandela,
inauguration address, Pretoria, May 10, 1994;
page 13: Dr. Patrick Dixon, *The Genetic Revolution*,
Kingsway Publications, 1993; page 20: *The
Independent*, September 30, 1998; page 23: quoted
in *Chronicle of the Year 1996*, Dorling Kindersley,
1997; page 26: *Antony Gormley*, Phaidon Press,
1995; page 34: Nick Bitel, on behalf of athlete
Dougie Walker, in *The Guardian*, April 1, 1999.

Contents

A Look at...

...in the '90s

A LOOK AT
THE NEWS
IN THE '90s

In 1990 the news seemed hopeful in many ways. The Cold War (long-term hostility between the Western capitalist countries and the communist bloc) had ended. People in the former USSR and Eastern Europe were beginning to enjoy new political freedoms. They hoped that economic change would bring a better life.

▷ *Residents of a black township east of Johannesburg line up to vote in South Africa's first all-race elections, April 1994.*

In South Africa, where blacks had waged a long struggle for equal rights against an oppressive white government, the majority of people were looking forward to building a new society based on justice for all. In 1990, Nelson Mandela and other African National Congress (ANC) leaders were freed from prison. In the country's first general election in 1994, Mandela became president.

On becoming president of South Africa, Nelson Mandela said:

"The time for the healing of wounds has come, the moment to bridge the chasms that divide us has come, the time to build is upon us."

War in the Gulf

The general optimism did not last long. In the summer of 1990, Iraq, an Islamic country led by dictator Saddam Hussein, invaded Kuwait. Hussein claimed that Kuwait's territory rightfully belonged to Iraq, but the invasion sparked an international crisis. In January 1991, U.S., British, French, Egyptian, and other forces, acting with United Nations Security Council approval, launched Operation Desert Storm, to remove Iraqi forces from Kuwait.

▷ *As the Iraqis retreated from Kuwait, they set fire to Kuwait's oil wells. Two Kuwaitis survey the damage.*

Hussein declared it would be "the mother of all battles," but could not match the weaponry and power of those ranged against him. Some 50,000 Iraqi soldiers were killed in the war.

Having driven the Iraqis from Kuwait, the allied leaders called a halt. They set up and patrolled "no-fly zones" within Iraq, to contain Hussein and hoped the Iraqi people would overthrow him. But he ruthlessly held on to power. In the following years, despite sanctions that isolated Iraq from world trade, UN inspectors found evidence that Hussein was stockpiling nuclear and chemical weapons. NATO planes bombed suspected Iraqi arms factories in 1998, but Hussein remained, and the Iraqi people continued to suffer.

The end of the USSR

Mikhail Gorbachev, leader of the USSR, had helped modernize his country and end the Cold War. But his own people blamed him for the food shortages, uncertainty, and loss of world power status that followed. Communist hardliners were also against Gorbachev's efforts to bring more openness and change to the USSR. In August 1991 they tried to seize power. Soldiers held Gorbachev and his wife captive in their vacation home in Crimea, while tanks moved into Moscow. Boris Yeltsin, the President of Russia, urged people in Moscow to resist the hardliners' coup, and in two days it collapsed. Gorbachev returned to power. By the end of 1991 the

▷ *Moscow, August 1991: Boris Yeltsin urges support for Gorbachev against the hardliners' coup.*

USSR had been dissolved and Gorbachev resigned, thrusting Yeltsin into prominence. Some republics had broken away to form independent countries, but other regions—including Chechnya—remained tied to Russia. In 1994 Yeltsin sent his army to intervene against a separatist uprising in Chechnya. After two years of fighting, with 30,000 lives lost, a treaty was patched together, but Chechnya remained unstable.

With the Communist Party out of power in Russia, Yeltsin introduced drastic reforms to the economy, such as lifting state controls on prices. Unemployment and crime increased. By 1998 Russia was deep in debt, and the ruble was devalued. People's savings were almost worthless, and many worked without pay for months and even years.

Profile

Slobodan Milosevic

A communist leader in Yugoslavia in the 1980s, Milosevic rose to power as the spokesman for Serbian nationalism, as ethnic strife between Serbs, Croats, and Muslims erupted in 1991. The fighting continued throughout the decade, strengthening Milosevic's position as a key regional figure. Although his country was in ruins following the Kosovo conflict, and despite being indicted for war crimes by a UN tribunal, Milosevic maintained his position as president.

Yugoslavia

In 1990 Yugoslavia was a country made up of six republics (Slovenia, Croatia, Bosnia, Serbia, Montenegro, and Macedonia) and two provinces (Kosovo and Vojvodina), held together under a communist system formed after World War II.

In 1991, Slovenia and Croatia declared independence. Serbian leader Slobodan Milosevic, who controlled the Yugoslav federal army, opposed them. The situation was complex because people of different ethnic backgrounds lived side by side, in different proportions, in each republic. Some people of Serbian origin in Croatia formed paramilitary units and called on the federal army for support. Milosevic's forces attacked both Croatia and Slovenia. Similar strife spread to Bosnia Herzegovina, where a large Muslim population came under Serb attack.

The nationalism and hatred that had been stirred up led to what was called "ethnic cleansing"—the forced driving out of local populations, accompanied by appalling cruelty. Ancient cities such as Vukovar in Croatia and Sarajevo in Bosnia were besieged and shelled.

▽ *April 1999: Ethnic Albanians, driven from their homes in Kosovo, arrive in Albania.*

▷ In central Africa, in 1994, conflict broke out between the Hutu and Tutsi peoples of Rwanda. Whole villages of Tutsi were massacred (right). Hutus fled the country, fearing retaliation, and vast refugee camps formed. As the decade closed, famine and disease stalked the once green and productive land.

Although the IRA continued a bombing campaign to try to end British rule in Northern Ireland, a slow peace process began, partly inspired by events in South Africa. In 1996, when talks broke down, the IRA detonated huge bombs at Canary Wharf, London, and in Manchester. U.S. Senator George Mitchell helped the Irish and British governments, loyalists, republicans and others resume their difficult negotiations. The Good Friday Agreement was signed in 1998 and, in referendums, people in both Northern Ireland and the Irish Republic voted in favor of it.

The European Community (EC) tried to negotiate peace, but numerous ceasefires were broken. In 1994, NATO planes went into offensive action for the first time, against Serb planes, to protect a no-fly zone created by the UN over Bosnia. In 1995 an uneasy peace agreement was signed in Dayton, Ohio. An international force was sent to police the ceasefire in Bosnia. Some leaders responsible for atrocities were declared guilty of war crimes.

In 1998 trouble flared again in the province of Kosovo, where the majority of people were of Albanian origin and supported some form of independence. Serb paramilitaries drove Kosovo Albanians from their homes and thousands were beaten or killed. In March 1999, NATO began a controversial air war against Serbia, to defend Kosovo Albanians. On June 9, the Serbs surrendered.

A long road to peace
International efforts to broker peace in two long-running conflicts—in Ireland and in the Middle East—saw former enemies at last accepting the need to listen to one another.

△ President Bill Clinton congratulates Israel's Prime Minister Yitzhak Rabin (left) and Palestine Liberation Organization (PLO) leader Yasser Arafat on the Oslo Accords, 1993. In 1995 Rabin was assassinated by a Jewish extremist opposed to the peace process. The process slowed, and the Oslo Accords expired in 1998 without the expected creation of a Palestinian nation.

A global economy

It became clear that, in several important respects, we all live in one world. International trading and the computerization of banks and stock exchanges meant that money and investment could be moved quickly around the world. Some multinational companies were richer and more powerful than many countries. They concentrated manufacturing in poorer countries, where people would work for lower wages. Consequently manual workers in other countries found it hard to get jobs.

In the mid-1990s Japan's economy began to falter. Then things started to go wrong in the countries of Southeast Asia (previously called "tiger" economies, because they had grown so strong so fast), and in 1998 Russia lurched into economic crisis. Fear of worldwide recession grew, bringing more unemployment and poverty. But the U.S. and European economies remained relatively strong. In 1999, the world's seven richest nations forgave some of the debts owed to them by developing nations, in order to boost growth in these countries.

...Newsflash...

Hong Kong, June 30, 1997. On the stroke of midnight, local time, Great Britain handed Hong Kong over to China, ending more than 150 years of colonial rule. At a ceremony held in torrential rain, Governor Chris Patten appealed to China to allow full democratic rights to the people of this booming capitalist city. China currently boasts "one country, two systems." Its Special Economic Zones are run on capitalist lines, but the rest of the country is communist. Despite uncertainty about their future, the Chinese population of Hong Kong celebrated through the night.

Human rights

Native Americans, the Inuit in Canada, and the aboriginal people in Australia won greater political rights and recognition of the harm

Profile

Aung San Suu Kyi

In 1988 the people of Burma rose against their military rulers. Aung San Suu Kyi led the pro-democracy movement. As the campaign grew, the generals panicked and arrested her. Still, when elections were held, her National League for Democracy won 82 percent of the vote. The generals then arrested members of parliament and killed demonstrators. In 1991 Suu Kyi was awarded the Nobel Peace Prize for her bravery. However, she remained under house arrest all through the 1990s. Crowds gathered at her gate, and she spoke out when she could.

◁ *In 1998, 9,000 people were killed when Hurricane Mitch tore through Nicaragua and Honduras, causing floods, mudslides, and tidal waves. Roads and bridges, like this one on the main road into Managua, were washed away, making it difficult for relief workers to get through.*

There were floods in the Netherlands, Belgium, northwest Germany, and northeast France in 1995. And eastern Germany was devastated in 1997, when the Oder River burst its banks. Bangladesh suffered particularly bad floods in 1991 and 1998.

done when their land was colonized by Europeans. In the 1990s, multinational companies were likened to the old colonial powers. In Colombia and Brazil they were accused of trampling on human rights and polluting the environment. In Nigeria, oil companies collaborated with a harsh military government to exploit Ogoniland. Ken Saro-Wiwa led local people in protest. When he and eight of his fellows were executed in 1995, there was international outcry.

A changing climate

Most of the warmest years of the century were in the 1990s. Manmade chemicals in the atmosphere were blamed for causing global warming, which contributed to a series of record climate events. The Mississippi River saw its worst floods ever in 1993, with 20 million acres under water. Parts of Egypt and Italy were deluged in 1994, leaving hundreds dead.

El Niño

Warming in the Pacific Ocean in 1997 (a periodic effect known as "El Niño") caused problems far away. In Indonesia, El Niño was followed by a drought, made worse by the burning of forests to clear land. For weeks, thick smog covered Borneo, Indonesia, and Malaysia.

▷ *In September 1997 children in Kuala Lumpur, Malaysia, wore masks to protect them against breathing in harmful smog.*

Profile

Diana, Princess of Wales

After the end of her unhappy marriage to Prince Charles, the Princess of Wales became a popular ambassador worldwide. Among other good causes, she worked for people with AIDS, and in 1996 she traveled to Bosnia and Angola to publicize the campaign against landmines. In August 1997 she died in a car crash. Thousands expressed their grief by leaving flowers and letters outside her home in London, and millions watched her funeral. In an extraordinary speech, her brother, Earl Spencer, criticized both the press and the royal family for ill-treating her.

△ Angola, February 1997: Princess Diana talks with landmine victims—a young girl and two former soldiers.

European Union

In 1992, the 12 countries of the European Community signed the Maastricht Treaty. This moved them closer toward economic and monetary union. The Danish people opposed this in a referendum, but changed their decision in 1993. Conservative ministers in Great Britain opposed closer ties with Europe, causing rifts in the government. In 1995, Austria, Finland, and Sweden joined the European Community, but Norway decided not to, so there were then 15 members in all.

▽ French President François Mitterrand (left) and German Chancellor Helmut Kohl led moves toward European integration. In 1993 a "single market" was created. This enabled goods and workers to move freely among EC countries.

...Newsflash...

Brussels, January 1, 1999. A new currency, the euro, comes into use in 11 European countries today. Great Britain and Denmark have opted out, while Sweden and Greece were not ready. At first, the euro will be used only for official transactions among banks. Coins and notes will be issued in 2002, replacing national currencies.

A new era

In Great Britain, on May 1, 1997, there was a landslide election victory for the Labor Party. Tony Blair became the youngest prime minister in 185 years. He promised to raise standards in schools and to reform the House of Lords. There were 119 women members of parliament in the House of Commons, by far the highest number ever. After referendums, Scotland gained its own parliament, and Wales an assembly.

In France, Lionel Jospin led the socialists to victory in 1997. A year later, a coalition of Social Democrats and the Green Party came to power in Germany. For the first time ever, the major countries of Europe had generally left-of-center governments and a new generation of leaders born since World War II.

The Clinton years

In 1992 Bill Clinton defeated George Bush to become president of the United States. The first Democrat president for 12 years, he was especially popular with women and black voters. The economy grew steadily, more people had jobs, and crime was reduced. However, a Republican Party majority in Congress blocked

...Newsflash...

Littleton, Colorado, April 21, 1999. When two teenagers walked into Columbine High School yesterday, shooting a teacher and 12 students dead before killing themselves, they left this town numb with horror. As after previous massacres, the National Rifle Association stated that people, not guns, are to blame. Some citizens and politicians want stricter gun control laws. Others blame the entertainment industry for its depictions of violence.

◁ *Tony Blair with South African President Nelson Mandela. After a general election in June 1999, Mandela retired. The new president was Thabo Mbeki.*

Clinton's attempts to reform health care, introduce gun controls, and curb the powerful tobacco industry. In 1998 the Republicans impeached the president after he lied under oath about his affair with White House worker Monica Lewinsky. The Senate narrowly backed Clinton, and he remained in office.

▷ *At President Clinton's impeachment trial in February 1999, the Senate considered videotaped recordings of the president being questioned by the Grand Jury.*

A LOOK AT
SCIENCE and TECHNOLOGY
IN THE '90s

In the 1990s, scientific research was aimed at learning more about DNA, the chief material in chromosomes. DNA carries the code that gives each living thing its particular characteristics.

Understanding DNA makes it possible to change or control those characteristics, or even to produce clones (exact copies) of living things from material in their cells. These developments raised ethical questions, since they gave humans the means to act upon nature in an entirely new way.

Mapping the genome

The total of the genetic material in a living thing is called its genome. The sequence in which this material is arranged makes a master plan for each individual life form—animal, plant, or microbe.

...Newsflash...

San Francisco, June 11, 1999. Dr. Francis Collins, head of the Human Genome Project (HGP), announced today that 90 percent of "the blueprint of human beings" will be finished by 2000, five years earlier than the original goal. Started in 1990, the HGP aimed to identify all 80,000 or so genes and determine the exact code inside each, a total of about 3 billion fragments that make up human DNA. This information will allow doctors to screen people for serious diseases, including cancer and heart disease.

Profile

Dolly the Sheep

In 1997, researchers in Edinburgh, Scotland, announced that they had produced the first ever clone of an adult animal. They took a single cell from an adult sheep and placed its genetic material in an unfertilized ovum (egg cell) that had been stripped of its own DNA. This was then placed inside a female sheep, who became its surrogate (replacement) mother. When the baby sheep was born, it was an exact copy of the sheep from which the original cell had been taken. They named her Dolly, and she quickly became the world's most photographed animal.

▽ *A forensic scientist takes a blood sample from some clothing, to make an "autorad(iograph)" of its DNA. Autorads are used in a similar way to fingerprints.*

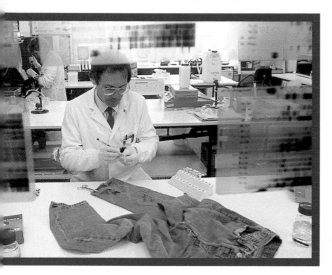

The process of working out the DNA sequence is called "mapping." First, scientists mapped the DNA of single-cell organisms, including yeast and certain bacteria that cause illness in humans. In December 1998 they revealed that they had mapped a multicelled organism for the first time. In 1990, scientists from many countries began a project to map the *human* genome.

▷ *These melons have been genetically modified to give off less gas than they do naturally (the tubes are checking this). The melons now ripen more slowly and so last longer.*

Using genetic knowledge

The uses of knowledge about genetics became clear as the decade progressed. The police identified criminals from DNA in a single hair or traces of blood or saliva. The precise genes associated with certain inherited illnesses were identified; this led to the development of more reliable medical tests and treatment. But such advances raised questions too. Would it spoil a person's life to know that he or she carried a hidden disease—especially if there was no cure? Would insurance companies expect people to have genetic tests before taking out health or life insurance?

Genetically modified crops

Farmers in the United States, China, Argentina, and Canada began to grow genetically modified soya, cotton, and corn, on a large scale. They used seeds produced

❝ ❞

In his book *The Genetic Revolution*, Dr. Patrick Dixon urged all people to become informed.

"If we do not take control of advancing gene technology now, then it will take control of us by changing the very roots of our society and our being."

and patented by chemical companies. Other countries held back. They were concerned that genetically modified foods could harm human or animal health, and that pollen from these crops might contaminate other crops or wildlife.

▷ *Greenpeace activists in France cut down genetically modified corn, September 1998.*

Some genetically modified seeds were "suicide seeds:" they were made with a terminator gene inside so that the next generation of seeds would be sterile. This meant that farmers would have to buy new seeds each year rather than saving their own. Before long, could the world's major crops all be under the control of a handful of private firms? As the decade ended, farmers in India and Brazil campaigned against being forced to use genetically modified seeds.

Food scares

People were also suspicious about new methods of food production for other reasons. Scientists had disagreed about whether BSE, a terrible disease that broke out in British cattle, could be passed to humans through eating beef. In 1996 they realized it could, and that some people had died as a result. Hundreds of thousands of cows had to be killed.

In the United States and 16 other countries, cows were regularly injected with BST, a man-made hormone, to increase the amount of milk they produced. In Europe use of the hormone was banned. It was said to damage the animals' health and pose a threat to human health, too.

Computers and the Internet

All through the 1990s, computers brought changes to the ways in which people lived and worked. Businesses and public services relied more and more on computers, linked through complex networks, to handle vast amounts of information. Instead of working in small local offices or banks, more people worked in large call centers dealing with telephone calls from customers far and wide.

◁ *Billionaire chairman of Microsoft Bill Gates (left) stands by as TV show host Jay Leno helps him launch his new Microsoft system, Windows 95, in August of 1995.*

Computers were vital to international trade, speeding up the way money and stocks were moved around. Since so many workers were expected to be computer-literate, schools increasingly taught information technology. At home, people used personal computers to get on the Internet and to send E-mail.

As technology developed, certain companies became famous for particular applications. IBM had led the way with spreadsheets and Macintosh with desk-top publishing. In the 1990s the dominant company was Microsoft. Its distinctive product was a versatile software system known as "Windows," which could be used with all IBM-compatible computers. In 1998, other companies challenged Microsoft in the U.S. courts, for blocking fair competition.

The Y2K and "Millennium Bug"

Another problem was far more troublesome. Y2K arose because of the coming change of dates in the year 2000. Many computers used only the last two digits of a four-digit year date. They would be likely to misinterpret the date "00;" as "1900" instead of "2000," this could cause whole systems to crash. The potential problem and the chaos that might follow had been recognized for years. But efforts to put matters right only gathered pace as the year 2000 approached. They involved reprogramming computer systems around the world and cost billions of dollars.

◁ *Buzz Lightyear (left) and Woody were two characters in* **Toy Story**, *the first feature-length film to be created entirely by computer animation, 1995.*

Bugs and viruses

In 1992, many computer users first became aware of the dangers of computer viruses. These could enter a computer's central system through contact with material from another computer. The bug then destroyed information stored on the computer's hard disk. In 1992 the Michelangelo virus did exactly this to many computers across the world. In 1999, two new viruses, named Melissa and Chernobyl, caused significant damage worldwide.

Movies and TV

Developments in the way computers could transform images meant that photographs and film could be manipulated in new and convincing ways. These techniques were used to enhance the original special effects in the *Star Wars* films, reissued in 1997, and to make the film *Babe*.

By the end of the 1990s digital television created the potential for a better-quality TV picture and sound. It meant more channels, though not necessarily better programs.

...Newsflash...

Houston, Texas, August 8, 1996. NASA announced today "a startling discovery that points to the possibility that a primitive form of microscopic life may have existed on Mars more than three billion years ago." Tests on a meteorite believed to have come from Mars showed fossil evidence of a primitive bacteria. Other scientists questioned the conclusion.

▷ *Comet Hale Bopp glides over Varna, Bulgaria, March 12, 1997. The comet was clearly visible through much of the northern hemisphere at dawn and dusk during March 1997. Named after two astronomers, it is four times larger than the famous Halley's Comet.*

▽ *Gas pillars in the Eagle Nebula— an image sent to earth by the Hubble Space Telescope in November 1995.*

Exploration of space

The United States and Russia still led the exploration of space, but now it was on a more cooperative basis. Astronauts from both countries worked on the space station *MIR*. In June 1997 there was concern when a supply ship collided with the elderly *MIR*, damaging the solar panels that provided power. Three astronauts were stranded in darkness with little oxygen. But they managed to make repairs. In 1998 the first module of a new international space station— the U.S.-financed, Russian-built *Zarya*—was launched.

Extraordinarily detailed images of events in space were provided by the Hubble Space Telescope, launched in 1990 to study the origin of the universe. There was also excitement when NASA's *Pathfinder* probe landed on Mars on July 4, 1997. It transmitted pictures of the planet's surface, but found no proof that life had ever existed there.

Transportation and technology

Because of concern about the pollution caused by car fumes, low-pollution cars using gas and batteries combined were being developed. Some people believed that fuel-cell electric cars were just a few years away. These would use hydrogen from methanol to produce an electric current. Some new vehicles contained tracking systems that informed the driver of road conditions ahead. But governments increasingly acknowledged the need to develop high-quality public transportation as an alternative to cars. France led the way with its fabulous high-speed trains. In 1999, Amtrak announced that it was building 20 high-speed electric trains, named Acelas, for its Boston–New York–Washington routes.

The use of cellular phones became widespread in the 1990s. But even in Italy, where cell phones were wildly popular, conflicts arose over the construction of cell phone transmitters. In 1999, smart phones—a wireless phone with text and Internet capabilities—were introduced and seen as the next wave of telecommunications. Smart phones can handle phone calls, hold addresses, take voice mail, access information on the Internet, and send and receive E-mail and fax transmissions. Industry analysts estimated that 1.5 million smart phones would be in use in the United States by 2002.

▽ With so many people on the move, mobile phones were used widely. However, evidence was gathered that showed constant use could cause headaches and even serious brain disease.

...Newsflash...

May 6, 1994. Trains are now running through the Channel Tunnel! Having opened a passenger terminal at London's Waterloo Station, Queen Elizabeth II traveled through the Tunnel to join President Mitterrand for a ribbon-cutting ceremony in France. The tunnel is a huge feat of engineering and technology. It was in October 1990 that the drillers from both countries first broke through with a 2-in. (5-cm) pilot hole. Two months later they met face to face. The high-speed train journey on Eurostar from London to Paris takes just three hours. Cars and trucks do not drive through but are transported on "le Shuttle."

A LOOK AT
FASHION
IN THE '90s

After the excesses of the previous decade, minimalism became the major theme in 1990s fashion. Most clothes were understated, and the exaggerated shoulder pads and power dressing of the 1980s were definitely out. Women's clothes were less structured and the fabrics more tactile.

In the mid-1990s some dresses were even deliberately made to look like lingerie, and the pants suit for women returned. In 1998, skirts for men appeared—though only a few were brave enough to wear them.

Making a statement
Young women wore tight, figure-revealing tops, with 1960s-style miniskirts; or with floating Hippie-style skirts or trousers, cut low to sit below the waist rather than on it. With these clothes often went long, loose hair styles. Many also wore rugged-looking footwear, seeming to state that girls could be anything they chose to be.

△ Fleece jackets and miniature backpacks turned the outward-bound look into city fashion.

New fabrics
Softer, body-revealing styles were achieved partly by the use of new stretchy, shiny fabrics containing Lycra.

The fashion-conscious bought fleece items—soft, unlined jackets made from synthetic fabric, which combined snug warmth with light weight. Developed

◁ Doc Martens boots (originally made as strong black leather working boots with reinforced toes) became a fashion item for young men and women. These dancers were part of the publicity for the opening of a store selling nothing but "Docs," in every imaginable color.

Profile

Miuccia Prada

Miuccia Prada transformed her family's business into one of the world's most successful fashion companies. She scored her first great success in 1985, when Prada nylon tote bags and backpacks became a status symbol. The elegant minimalism of Prada's clothing line set the tone for 1990s fashion, and her prominence was unmistakable when Drew Barrymore and Uma Thurman arrived at the 1995 Oscars in Prada gowns.

◁ *Miuccia Prada's best decision was in branching out from solely leather goods to women's fashion.*

originally for sportswear and outdoor pursuits, fleece had the great advantage of being machine-washable. As part of this casual, comfortable style, most people owned a pair of running shoes, and the fashion status that they achieved in the late 1980s lingered on.

New designers

During the 1990s, young designers from around the world took charge at the famous European fashion houses: British newcomers John Galliano at Christian Dior and Alexander McQueen at Givenchy; Americans Tom Ford at Gucci, Marc Jacobs at Louis Vuitton, and Michael Kors at Céline; and Belgian Martin Margiela at Hermés.

Fashion for everyone

Designers from Helmut Lang to Tommy Hilfiger were influenced by street fashion. The hip-hop look—which began with inner-city teenagers wearing jeans, logo shirts, and windbreakers, all oversized and in primary colors— became mainstream fashion in the United States.

◁ *One of Alexander McQueen's concepts for the London Fashion Show, 1997*

Fashion in the 1990s also became big business, with brand-name designers like Ralph Lauren, Calvin Klein, and Donna Karan creating design empires that went beyond clothing to include perfume, towels, underwear, and even furniture.

Meanwhile, The Gap and its sister stores Banana Republic and Old Navy turned such basics as the T-shirt and chinos into must-have clothes.

Models and advertising

Top fashion models such as Linda Evangelista, Cindy Crawford, Naomi

Assessing the changes in the fashion marketplace, *New York Times* reporter Anne-Marie Schiro observed in 1991

"The latest buzzword for fashion isn't mini or maxi or stretch. It's globalization."

▷ *Super-models like Claudia Schiffer were paid huge sums in return for adding their names and images to all kinds of products.*

Campbell, Kate Moss, and Claudia Schiffer became rich and famous. But some people criticized magazines and agencies for the fact that models were always unusually tall, super-thin, and in some cases quite ill-looking.

Profile

Naomi Campbell

Supermodels were a small group of models who became international stars, famous way beyond the world of fashion. Great Britain's Naomi Campbell was the only black woman among them. She had a winning personality and extremely long legs, and looked as good in glamorous catwalk oufits as in street-style clothes. Naomi was 19 when she appeared on the front cover of *Vogue* magazine in 1990. She rapidly became very famous. High session fees and advertising contracts made her extremely wealthy. A book about her life is titled *The Rise and Rise of the Girl from Nowhere.*

Minimalism

Fashion in the 1990s covered the extremes, ranging from grunge and slipdresses to utility chic and casual Fridays. Rages came and went—the monastic look, Gucci's slit skirt, platform shoes—but the overwhelming trend was in the direction of minimalism. Casting aside the flashy clothing of the 1980s, designers promoted a clean, modern look. The most influential styles of the decade included the minimalist designs of Helmut Lang and Miuccia Prada and the futuristic designs of Japan's Yohji Yamamoto. For accessories, minimal was also the word, as seen in handbags by Kate Spade and Prada.

Everyday Clothes

Sportwear remained popular, however, with striped warm-up pants, baseball caps, and high-tech sneakers often spotted both on trendy urban streets and in suburban shopping malls. Casual clothing became more

common in the workplace as businesses relaxed their dress codes.

Body-piercing and tattoos

Body-piercing and tattoos were popular among young people, especially girls. Studs decorated ears, eyebrows, noses, and navels. Some people even went as far as getting their tongues pierced.

...Newsflash...

Miami Beach, Florida, July 15, 1997. The fashion world loses one of its stars when 50-year-old Gianni Versace is murdered outside his Miami Beach mansion by fugitive spree killer Andrew Cunanan. Versace's clothes were considered a symbol of glamor and boldness, and he had many celebrity clients and friends, including Madonna, Elton John, and Princess Diana.

◁ *Some people chose to have a stud or ring in their navels.*

▷ *Tennis star André Agassi made his own fashion statement on the court. His shorts were baggy, in the style of trousers popular among many young men in the United States. His shirts were cut short at the front to show a flash of stomach when he served.*

A LOOK AT
MUSIC
IN THE '90s

Rock 'n' roll continued its evolution in the 1990s, with established bands such as U2 and R.E.M leading the way, and exciting new artists—including Smashing Pumpkins, Pavement, and Beck—creating new sounds. The real story of the decade, however, was the tremendous rise in the popularity of hip-hop and country, which found fans beyond their traditional audiences. Another trend was the emergence of women songwriters.

At the start of the 1990s, "grunge," which owed its spirit to '70s punk, emerged. Nirvana and Pearl Jam were popular and influential grunge bands. Nirvana's 1991 hit "Smells Like Teen Spirit" expressed the frustrations of contemporary youth. The 1994 suicide of Nirvana's Kurt Cobain marked the loss of the most important rock songwriter of the time.

Although some rappers in the 1990s, such as Tupac Shakur and Snoop Doggy Dogg, continued to be criticized for the violent content in their lyrics, Puff Daddy, Missy Elliott, the Fugees, and other artists produced hip-hop songs

▽ *Noel and Liam Gallagher of Oasis, at a concert in 1996*

Profile

Michael Jackson

Michael Jackson (seen here in 1997) was a supreme showman, singer, and dancer. In 1991 he launched his single and video *Black or White* and began a world tour. His skin was white and his features had changed. In a rare TV interview with Oprah Winfrey, he said his pale skin was caused by a disease. But his personal behavior remained secretive and strange. He issued *History*, a double album and video costing $50 million to make, in 1995. In 1996 he made a video in the slums of Rio de Janeiro, *They Don't Really Care About Us*.

Profile

The Spice Girls

British girl band the Spice Girls topped the singles charts in 28 countries in 1996. Their energetic songs and dance routines became hugely famous. Individually they were known as Scary, Sporty, Posh, Baby, and Ginger Spice. Ginger Spice (Geri Halliwell) left the group in 1998, and later released a solo album. She was appointed to work for the United Nations as a goodwill ambassador. The other Spice Girls carried on, even after two announced that they were having babies.

that appealed to fans of all races, ages, and locales. Many bands, such as the Red Hot Chili Peppers, blended rap, rock 'n' roll, jazz, and other influences to carve out their own distinctive sounds. The beat at dance clubs was dominated by various styles of music— acid house, trip-hop, industrial, and techno— and 1970s disco and funk enjoyed a revival.

▷ *Puff Daddy (left) in Los Angeles, 1998*

Boy and girl bands

The biggest worldwide stars were the Spice Girls, with their "girl power." Boy bands— including Hanson, Boyz II Men, Backstreet Boys, NSYNC, and 98 Degrees—also struck it big, particularly with teen audiences.

" "

In his 1997 book, *Fight the Power: Rap, Race, and Reality*, Chuck D. wrote:

"My focus was not on boasting about myself or battling brothers on the microphone. I wanted to rap about battling institutions, and bringing the condition of black people worldwide to a respectable level."

Decade of the woman

Women musicians came into their own in the 1990s. Leading the way was 1980s star Madonna, whose songs and style matured in the 1990s. Many female singer/songwriters—including Alanis Morisette, Sarah McLachlan, Jewel, Sinead O'Connor, Lauryn Hill, Sheryl Crow, Mary Chapin Carpenter, Queen Latifah, and Alison Krause—expressed their viewpoints in pop, rock, rap, country, and folk songs. Several girl bands, or bands fronted by women, struck it big in the 1990s, including Hole (led by Kurt Cobain's widow, Courtney Love), the Breeders, Belly, and Luscious Jackson. Pop divas Whitney Houston, Celine Dion, and Maria Carey dominated the airwaves, and Iceland's Björk mesmerized fans worldwide with

△ Talented and original female singer Björk, seen here in 1996, is from Iceland.

her distinctive voice. Jazz pianist and singer Diane Krall and classical stars Cecilia Bartoli and Nadja Salerno-Sonnenberg enjoyed critical and commercial success.

Country stars

New stars—including Garth Brooks, LeeAnn Rimes, and Shania Twain—gave country music a more pop-oriented sound, helping it to reach a much larger audience. Traditionally more popular in southern, western, and rural areas, country music expanded its appeal into urban areas; country-music radio stations even succeeded in large northern cities. Such bands as Uncle Tupelo, Wilco, and Son Volt blended alternative rock and traditional country music to create an entirely new sound known as alt-country.

The year of the Latin singer

In the late 1990s, music industry forecasters predicted that Latin music would be the next big thing, and two phenomenally popular artists made their prediction come true in 1999. Ricky Martin released his first English-language album, Ricky Martin, and crowds of adoring fans flocked to concerts to see the hip-swinging singer perform his hit, "Livin' la Vida Loca." Actress Jennifer Lopez showed her versatility

◁ The 1998 Danish grammy winners Aqua had a huge hit with their ironic song "Barbie Girl."

...Newsflash...

September 14, 1997. Elton John's recording of "Candle in the Wind," released yesterday, sold 600,000 copies in one day! This makes it the fastest-selling single ever. Elton John rewrote the song, which he had originally penned in memory of Marilyn Monroe, as a memorial to Diana, Princess of Wales, who had been a personal friend. He performed the song at her funeral in Westminster Abbey, accompanying himself on the piano. All the money raised by sales of the record are to go to the Diana Memorial Fund.

△ *Young violinists Nigel Kennedy and Vanessa Mae (above) did not conform to the usual ways of classical musicians. Their flamboyant looks and style gave a new image to the music they performed.*

with her chart-topping album, *On the 6.* Their triumphs recalled the pop success of Latin music earlier in the decade: Tejano singer Selena's 1995 album *Dreaming of You* and the 1996 international megahit "Macarena."

Outdoor music festivals
Outdoor music festivals remained popular with music fans. Woodstock '94 and Woodstock '99 revived the traditions of the first 1969 Woodstock rock festival, attracting thousands of music fans. Woodstock '99 made

headlines when the festival ended in a minor riot. Other popular music festivals in the decade included Lollapalooza (featuring mostly alternative rock bands), Lilith Fair (featuring women musicians), and The Fleadh (featuring Irish music).

◁ *Outdoor rock festivals grew larger and more commercial in the 1990s. Young people camped out, sometimes in appalling weather, to enjoy the music.*

A LOOK AT
ART and ARCHITECTURE
IN THE '90s

Painting seemed to take a back seat to other forms of visual art, such as sculpture and installations, in the 1990s.

In 1993, sixteen giant sculptures by Fernando Botero graced Park Avenue, New York City. In 1998, extraordinary, gigantic figures were created and paraded through the streets of Paris for the opening of the World Cup. In May 1999, New York City's Central Park was home to a large sculpture: an arrangement of false boulders that imitated the park's rocky outcroppings was installed. While making the sculpture, sculptor Andrea Zittel had to

British Sculptor Antony Gormley said:

"any piece of work in the late twentieth century has to speak to the whole world."

▷ *Ho, Pablo, Moussa, and Romeo, the figures paraded through Paris for the opening of the World Cup, represented the continents. Ho (right) symbolized Asia.*

redesign the boulders after realizing that daredevil skateboarders might get injured by using them as ramps.

Installations

Artists in the remaining communist countries gained greater worldwide recognition, and some used their art as a way to express political messages. Chinese multimedia artist Zhang Peili exhibited his video installations at respected museums and galleries worldwide, including New York City's Museum of Modern Art. His

"Uncertain Pleasure," for example, used close-up images of a man relentlessly scratching his body, reflecting the tension that exists between the joys and frustrations of modern urban life. Young Cuban installation artist Kcho makes sculpture from natural materials and found objects. His "Boat," a floor-to-ceiling pileup of bottles, tables, wood scraps, and a rowboat, commented on the flight of Cubans from their homeland on makeshift rafts.

Photography

The images of Brazilian photojournalist Sebastião Salgado captured the attention of the art world. His striking photographs of poor and downtrodden people in many countries were exhibited and acclaimed worldwide. American photographer William Wegman achieved commercial and artistic success with his series of photographs of his weimaraner dogs posed like humans in various settings.

△ *Inside the parliament (Reichstag) building in Berlin—with a new dome designed by architect Norman Foster. It reopened in 1999.*

Painting

Although many young artists were not working with paint, the Fractalist movement attracted such young painters as Pascal Dombis of France, Mexico's Miguel Chevalier, and Nancy Lorenz of the United States. Their abstract paintings resembled computer-generated images or patterns seen in close-up photographs of natural objects. The work of the Fractalists was first showcased in a 1998 exhibition by Nart, an Internet gallery.

British painter Damien Hirst achieved notoriety with his installations, sometimes featuring dead animals preserved in formaldehyde. American painter Peter Stanick made a splash by poking fun at art and artists. His cartoonlike paintings, recalling the work of 1960s artist Roy Lichtenstein, had titles like "That's art? It's just a dead shark" (aimed at Hirst) and "It looks like a child did it." In his eerie paintings, Zhang Xiaogang addressed the issues of China's Cultural Revolution (1966–76), which sought to eliminate many Chinese traditions.

◁ *Damien Hirst with one of his installations entitled "Mother and Child," at the Tate Gallery, London, 1995.*

Architecture

Some self-confident, highly original public buildings were built in the 1990s, including major museums and galleries. This was a change from the 1980s, when commercial buildings such as banks and shopping malls predominated. Architects experimented with how a building encloses space, and with the use of natural light. They used new materials and giddy, unexpected shapes.

Spain leads the way

Spain's economic and democratic progress was displayed when it hosted Expo '92 in Seville. A new city with bold architecture and gardens was developed on the island of Cartuja, plus a new airport and high-speed rail link with Madrid. Architect Ricardo Bofill designed the airport and the National Theater of Catalunya.

The world's highest buildings, the Petronas Towers in Kuala Lumpur, Malaysia, were completed shortly before the Asian economic crisis of August 1997. In the United States, new buildings at Arizona State University were praised, as were the Seattle Art Museum and the

...Newsflash...

Cleveland, Ohio, September 1, 1995. The grand opening of the Rock and Roll Hall of Fame Museum was held today. Designed by renowned architect I. M. Pei, the $92 million-dollar structure rises six stories above the Lake Erie waterfront in downtown Cleveland, where DJ Alan Freed gave the new music its name in the 1950s. The museum features exhibition halls, theaters, and a hall of fame featuring tributes to rock and roll's greatest artists.

▽ *In the Basque city of Bilbao, northern Spain, the futuristic Guggenheim Museum took shape. Covered in glittering titanium, it was immediately hailed as the masterpiece building of the twentieth century. The architect, Frank Gehry, also designed part of the Weisman Museum in Minneapolis.*

Profile

Norman Foster

Norman Foster's work won worldwide acclaim. His earlier British buildings, including Stansted Airport and the Sainsbury Gallery at the University of East Anglia, seemed to celebrate natural light and space. In the 1990s he designed the dome for Berlin's Reichstag and was chosen to design the new assembly for Wales. His American Air Museum at Duxford, Cambridgeshire, won an award in 1998. It was judged "a great big, clear-span building beautifully integrated into its flat landscape, cunningly daylit around its perimeter, and with a virtuoso roof ... from which the planes are suspended."

▷ *The Petronas Towers in Kuala Lumpur stand in a park designed to be a haven for tropical flora and fauna.*

Tennessee Aquarium in Chattanooga. In Australia, Gregory Burgess designed unusual unobtrusive buildings to be used as aboriginal cultural centers.

As the 1990s ended, Berlin was being transformed into a new capital city for Germany, perhaps a cultural center for all Europe. As well as the new parliament building (page 27), a new railroad station was taking shape—Europe's biggest—boasting a 1,410-ft. (430-m) glass concourse, 58 escalators, and 37 elevators. Meanwhile, in Great Britain, the coming of the 21st century was celebrated by the building of a Millennium Dome, designed by Richard Rogers, to look like a giant spacecraft that had landed close to the meridian at Greenwich, England.

A LOOK AT
SPORTS
IN THE '90s

Sports were more prominent in people's lives than ever. Millions watched sporting events, and, with a growing number of television channels, some dedicated entirely to sports, even minor sports found an audience. Football, tennis, baseball, and basketball became highly profitable industries. Famous teams were listed on the stock exchange. Sports management courses were popular in colleges, and careers opened up. Finally many people took part in sports as amateurs.

▷ At the Olympic Games in Atlanta, 1996, Kerri Strug was part of the U.S. Women's Gymnastics Team, which won gold.

Goodbye
Wayne Gretzky (hockey) Florence Griffith Joyner (track); Diego Maradona (soccer); John Elway (football); Steffi Graf (tennis)

Hello
Sammy Sosa (baseball); Mia Hamm (soccer); Venus Williams (tennis); Tara Lipinski (skating), Tiger Woods (golf)

Marathons
Men and women participated at all levels of ability in marathons held in cities around the world. Some were sponsored for charity. Some took part as disabled competitors. Among the winners, black African runners dominated, in the tradition of their Olympic successes in earlier decades. In the London marathon held in 1997, 29,000 competitors took part, a record for any race anywhere.

Soccer—worldwide
Thanks to satellite TV, famous teams such as Manchester United or Barcelona had fans as far away as Africa and China. As audiences grew, soccer changed from being a sport mainly of interest to working-class men. Grounds and facilities were improved, and the game became fashionable. During three World Cup finals in 1990, 1994, and 1998, it seemed that whole populations were caught up in following their national teams. Soccer even grew in the United States, which hosted the 1994 World Cup.

...Newsflash...

Pasadena, California, July 10, 1999. In front of 90,000 fans and a worldwide television audience estimated at one billion, the U.S. women's soccer team won the World Cup today, outscoring China on penalty kicks. The stadium erupted in cheers as Brandi Chastain clinched the title with the team's fifth kick. The event reportedly broke an attendance record for a women's sporting event in the United States.

▷ In the 1994 World Cup final, Italy's Roberto Baggio hangs his head after missing a penalty kick. This miss, in front of a 94,000-strong crowd in Pasadena, California, meant that Italy lost to Brazil.

Interest was especially high in communities in the United States where many people are originally from Italy or South America.

Top players and managers could command high salaries around the world. Big teams made fortunes from sponsorship and television broadcast rights. Professional soccer returned to the United States in 1996 as Major League Soccer, featuring top players from around the world,

Profile

Lance Armstrong

In the 1999 Tour de France, American cyclist Lance Armstrong won cycling's greatest race and gained the admiration of fans worldwide. Armstrong won the 2,292-mile race, one of the toughest events in sports, less than three years after doctors gave him only a 50-50 chance of living. In late 1996, he had contracted an aggressive cancer that spread to his lungs and brain. Armstrong endured major surgery and four rounds of chemotherapy. He dedicated his victory to other cancer survivors, whom he hoped would be inspired by his success.

◁ *Jonah Lomu storms forward in the All Blacks' match against England, 1997. An enormous man, Lomu was hard to stop!*

in South Africa meant that sports previously reserved for whites also had to accept change. Now South African teams were welcomed back into world sports.

In June 1995, South Africa hosted and won the Rugby World Cup. The South African team beat the New Zealand All Blacks—including star player Jonah Lomu—in a thrilling final. President Mandela joined the celebrations, as the colorful new South African flag was waved. It marked a unifying moment in a country where sports are almost a religion.

South Africa returns to world sports

Some of the political problems that bedeviled sports in earlier decades had faded. For years South African sports had been boycotted by other countries, because of the country's system of apartheid. The change of government

...Newsflash...

Baltimore, Maryland, September 6, 1995. Baseball all-star Cal Ripken Jr. played in his 2,131st consecutive game tonight to break the major-league record for consecutive games played, eclipsing the remarkable 56-year-old mark set by Yankees legend Lou Gehrig. Ripken hadn't been out of the Orioles' starting lineup since May 29, 1982.

Profile

Michael Jordan

Michael Jordan was the greatest basketball player and sports celebrity of the 1990s. Playing for the Chicago Bulls, Jordan led his team to three NBA championships (1991–93). His amazing athleticism and competitive spirit thrilled fans worldwide. After an unsuccessful attempt at becoming a major-league baseball player, Jordan returned to the Bulls and led them to three more NBA championships (1996–98). After winning an NCAA championship, two Olympic gold medals, and six NBA championships, Jordan retired in 1999.

Golden days in Atlanta

The 1996 Olympics, in Atlanta, Georgia, were the largest games ever. More than 11,000 athletes from 197 nations took part, and events were broadcast live to audiences around the world, who witnessed some record-breaking performances.

Kerri Strug competed with a damaged ankle to help the U.S. women's gymnastics team win its first ever gold. The effort earned Strug a reputation for dedication and selflessness as well as popularity. Nigeria became the first ever African team to win gold in the soccer competition, while Josia Thugwane, who won the men's marathon, was the first black South African to win Olympic gold.

Perhaps the most remarkable achievement was by Michael Johnson. The American sprinter electrified the world by becoming the first person in history to win gold medals in both the 200-meter and 400-meter races at the same Olympic Games. In the 200-meter dash, Johnson shattered his own world record with a time of 19.32.

Sports commentators asked:

"Have the Olympic Games become too big and too commercial? And now that sports like synchronized swimming and beach volleyball have been included, where will it all end?"

◁ *The 1994 Winter Olympics were held in Norway and brought 2 million visitors to the country—equal to half the country's population. Norway topped the medals table, and Norwegian speed skater Johann Koss set three new world records.*

◁ Cyclists in the 1998 Tour de France staged a strike in protest at the way the French police had taken some participants to the hospital for drug tests. Danish cyclist Bjarne Riis acted as spokesman.

Athletes challenged the accuracy of drug tests through the courts. One lawyer said:

"There is evidence that an adverse finding can be caused by nandrolone naturally occurring in the body, by supplements not on the banned list, or by meat products."

Problems with drugs

Unfortunately, some athletes resorted to taking drugs to boost their performances. Drug scandals nearly wrecked the famous Tour de France cycle race in 1998. Two notable athletes were marred by charges of drug use: Tennis star Petr Korda retired after being suspended for testing positive for performance-enhancing drugs, and the Olympic Committee stripped Irish swimmer Michelle Smith of her gold medals because she failed a drug test.

The effects of sudden fame and fast lifestyles also caused problems. Use of so-called recreational drugs interrupted the career of tennis player Jennifer Capriati. The drug and alcohol problems of baseball player Darryl Strawberry, football great Lawrence Taylor, and figure skater Oksana Baiul also made headlines.

▷ At just 21 years old, Eldrick "Tiger" Woods won the 1997 U.S. Masters, playing some of the finest golf ever seen. His was the best score in the competition's history, and he won by the biggest ever margin. His success was the more remarkable in a sport with very few non-white players.

Tennis

Supreme champion of the 1990s was Pete Sampras of the United States, with his serve and volley game. André Agassi and Goran Ivanisevic rose through the ranks, while Boris Becker was still a force to be reckoned with. There was concern that the game had been spoiled by new-style rackets. These made shots harder and faster, but reduced delicate "touch" play and the number and length of rallies. In response, tennis authorities altered the weight of the ball to slow it down.

Women's tennis overtook men's tennis in popularity, and the women players began to demand equal prize money. Martina Navratilova retired in 1994 with a career total of 167 singles titles. She had dominated the game for so long that three years later Martina Hingis, who had been named after Navratilova, won her first Wimbledon title! Up till then, Steffi Graf and Monica Seles led women's

△ In 1997, 16-year-old Martina Hingis from Switzerland became the youngest Wimbledon champion of the century. She also won the U.S. Open and Australian titles.

tennis. In a horrific incident in 1993, a crazed spectator stabbed Seles on court in Hamburg. She recovered and began a successful comeback two years later.

Baseball

In August 1994, baseball players in the United States went on strike for more pay. Team owners responded by calling off the whole season. In 1998, Roger Maris's 37-year-old home run record was broken by Sammy Sosa. He hit 66 for the Chicago Cubs. Mark McGwire of the St. Louis Cardinals then beat that with 70 home runs in one season.

...Newsflash...

New York, New York, April 18, 1999. Hockey immortal Wayne Gretzky played his final NHL game today, having previously announced that he would retire after the New York Rangers' final game of the season. In the Rangers 2-1 overtime loss to the Pittsburgh Penguins, Gretzky recorded his 1,963rd assist and 2,857th point of his illustrious career. In 21 seasons, Gretzky established 61 NHL records, captured ten scoring titles and nine most valuable player awards, and played on four Stanley Cup–championship teams. Gretzky will be remembered for his impact in broadening the appeal of hockey worldwide.

A LOOK AT
LEISURE and ENTERTAINMENT
IN THE '90s

In the 1990s more and more of the movies and television people watched, the books and magazines they read, and even the food they ate, were produced by huge multinational corporations.

One example was News International, owned by Rupert Murdoch. It controlled TV and film companies, newspapers, publishing houses, and sports teams around the world. There was concern that such monopolies threatened cultural diversity and freedom of expression.

American influence

Now that the Cold War was over, U.S. culture and products were more powerful than ever. The red Coca-Cola logo was said to be the world's most widely recognized symbol. Coca-Cola's arch-rival, Pepsi, spent $500 million on remarketing Pepsi in blue packaging. Theme restaurants such as Planet Hollywood, and the Rainforest Café, used their links with celebrities to attract customers, but by the end of the decade their success was fading. Fast-food corporation

△ An inflated figure of Ronald McDonald outside a new McDonald's in Beijing, 1994.

Profile

The Simpsons

The Simpsons, an inventive and very funny television cartoon series of the 1990s, took an ironic look at life in the United States. Homer Simpson worked at a nuclear plant. He was a glutton and a lazy, although loving, father. Marge, his wife, waged a losing battle to improve her family's manners. Bart, with his rude ways and constant search for thrills, was completely unlike his sisters, the high-achieving, wise, and intellectual Lisa and baby Maggie. *The Simpsons* was hugely popular with children and adults.

McDonald's grew at an astonishing rate, even opening outlets in Moscow and Beijing. The menu, no matter where, was based on sameness and limited choice. It was targeted at young people.

Some people resented the rise of fast-food culture, especially in France with its tradition of fine cooking. But even in France, hamburger outlets grew in number. In Europe and the United States, many more mothers needed jobs than ever before. Fewer people cooked at home from raw ingredients. The majority of homes acquired microwaves. Supermarkets sold more and more ready-made meals. At the same time, some people developed a "foodie" culture, drawing on the best of world cuisine. Top chefs became famous. Other celebrity chefs—such as Emeril Lagasse, Bobby Flay, and the Two Fat Ladies—had their own TV series, and their books were best-sellers.

...Newsflash...

May 12, 1999. The long-awaited Star Wars, Episode One: *The Phantom Menace* opened yesterday with dramatic results. Film studio 20th Century Fox reported that it broke the all-time high for one-day ticket sales in the United States and Canada, taking in $28.5 million. Director George Lucas had urged the studio to debut the film on a Wednesday so the Star Wars series' biggest supporters could see it first. Because yesterday was a work day, many die-hard fans played what has come to be known as "Wookie hooky."

▷ *Line dancing, 1998*

Dancing

A new craze, line dancing, caught on among people of all ages. It spread outward from the United States.

Some line dancers dressed up in Western-style clothes and boots; the moves involved cowboy-style heel-clicking and jumping. It was all great fun, and since everyone danced in a line, you didn't even need a partner!

Meanwhile a spectacular new show called *Riverdance* made Irish dancing popular. Performed to traditional music, Irish dancing involves fast footwork while the top half of the body stays upright and still.

△ In Riverdance, *a troupe of men and women danced with military precision, filling the stage with sound.*

Theme parks

During the 1990s theme parks, where families could spend days enjoying spectacular rides and exhibits, grew in size and number. Lego, makers of the popular toy, opened a Legoland in England, to match the one in Denmark. EuroDisney, later re-launched as Disneyland Paris, opened in France in 1992.

Engineers competed to build the world's biggest, most thrilling rides. They studied aspects of safety, and what forces the average human body can take without coming to harm. The Incredible Hulk Coaster, which can reach a speed of nearly 70 miles per hour (44 km/h), began operation at Universal Studios's Islands of Adventure theme park in May 1999.

◁ April 1992: *a parade during the opening of EuroDisney in Paris*

Shopping

Suburban shopping malls, common in the United States, had spread to Great Britain and Europe. In response, some local governments invested in revitalizing town centers, so that they would not become run-down and empty.

In the United States, TV shopping became popular. After seeing products described on cable shopping channels, such as QVC, or in hour-long commercials devoted to a single product (known as infomercials), people telephoned their orders, paying with credit cards. Shopping via the Internet was hailed as the wave of the future. It was now possible to order products online and have them delivered to your door. Online shopping got off to a slow start because many people worried about having their credit card details stolen. Security systems were developed, however, and online merchants attracted an increasing number of customers.

Computer games

Games could be played on home computers or via television sets with a console. The graphics became very sophisticated. Portable computer games such as Game Boy were popular too. In 1997, there was a craze for Tamagotchi "virtual pets." These were small computerized toys from Japan that had to be "fed" at regular intervals or else they would "die." As more homes went on-line, some people spent many hours a week surfing the Internet, or holding conversations via E-mail.

Exercise

Children were said to spend too much time in front of computer or television screens. They weren't as fit as children used to be. But parents were often unwilling to let children play outside or walk or ride bikes to school, because of the danger from high levels of traffic. Even so, many children did find places to enjoy the new craze, rollerblading, or ride their mountain bikes.

◁ Rollerblading was a new craze.

▷ *Leonardo Di Caprio and Kate Winslet struggle to escape the sinking Titanic. Like many films in the 1990s, Titanic made a second fortune for its producers when released on video.*

A revival of movies

The development of new multiscreen complexes helped movie audiences grow. However people often complained that only block-buster films, strongly "hyped" by producers and distributors, were shown. *Jurassic Park*, directed by Steven Spielberg, and *Titanic*, directed by James Cameron, broke box-office records with their thrilling special effects. Together with Disney animated films *Pocahontas* and *The Lion King*, they were soon released in video form for home viewing and led to lots of spin-off toys and merchandise.

One surprise hit was *Babe*, a film based on a children's story by Dick King-Smith. It used computerized imaging to make real animals appear to talk and act in a human way. *Forrest Gump*, starring Tom Hanks, used computer techniques to insert its hero into newsreels from recent history. Tom Hanks starred again in *Saving Private Ryan*, which was released in 1998. The film depicted with horrifying realism the Normandy landings that helped to end World War II. *Braveheart*, too, dealt with history and graphic battle scenes.

Profile

Nick Park

British animator Nick Park created Wallace and Grommit, whose adventures became Oscar-winning films. Wallace is a fussy Englishman who makes weird inventions, and Grommit is a comical dog with floppy ears. *Grand Day Out, The Wrong Trousers*, and other films were created frame by frame, using plasticine figures and detailed sets made to scale. In 1996 Wallace and Grommit had a real adventure when Nick Park left the figures by mistake in a New York taxicab. Happily, they were returned unharmed.

Goodbye

River Phoenix, actor; Rudolf Nureyev, ballet dancer; Roald Dahl, children's writer; Satyajit Ray, Indian filmmaker; Ted Hughes, poet

Hello

Leonardo Di Caprio, actor; Natalie Portman, actor; J. K. Rowling, writer; Sarah Michelle Gellar, actor; Savion Glover, dancer

In this case it was the story of William Wallace, a 13th-century Scottish hero who led a revolt against the English. The leading actor and director of *Braveheart*, Mel Gibson, became very popular among the Scots, who were seeking more independence from England in the 1990s.

In 1997 no fewer than nine Academy Awards (Oscars) went to *The English Patient*, a film based on a prize-winning novel. In 1999 a comedy, *Shakespeare in Love*, won seven Oscars.

...Newsflash...

New York, June 7, 1998. The Lion King edged out *Ragtime* tonight to win the 1998 Tony Award for best musical. Based on Disney's amazingly successful animated film, the play also took five other awards—for direction, choreography, lighting, sets, and costumes. "This is just spectacular, spectacular," director Julie Taymor exclaimed as she received a standing ovation early in the evening. *The Lion King* is playing at the New Amsterdam Theater, which reopened last year after Disney spent $34 million renovating it.

viewers, such as *Party of Five, Dawson's Creek*, and *Seventh Heaven*.

As well as these high-budget movies, some low-budget movies (often called "indies" because they were made independent of big Hollywood studios) included *Fargo, Trainspotting, Shine,* and *The Blair Witch Project*.

Television

Barney and *Teletubbies* were popular with small children, and animated programs such as *Rugrats* were for older children and adults. TV networks began airing more programs aimed at young

Books

British writer J. K. Rowling's *Harry Potter and the Chamber of Secrets* became an immediate hit in England in 1997, and it enjoyed a huge success in the United States. The book and its sequels dazzled readers with the adventures of a young boy attending Hogwarts School for Wizards and Witches.

◁ *Children everywhere flocked to see American child star Macaulay Culkin in the* Home Alone *movies.*

March 13 ▷ A crazed former scout leader, obsessed with guns, enters Dunblane primary school in Scotland and shoots 16 pupils, their teacher, and then himself dead.

March 25 ▷ Europe imposes a worldwide ban on the export of British beef. There is now proof of a link between BSE in cows and a new strain of fatal Creutzfeldt-Jakob disease in humans.

April 4 ▷ The so-called unabomber is arrested in a remote part of Montana. For 17 years the former math professor planted bombs in universities and computer stores.

August 28 ▷ The 15-year marriage of Prince Charles and Diana, Princess of Wales, ends in divorce. Charles denies that he intends to marry his long-term mistress Camilla Parker Bowles.

September 27 ▷ The Taliban introduce a fundamentalist Islamic state in Afghanistan.

1997

February 19 ▷ Deng Xiaoping, Chinese leader, dies at age 92. Jiang Zemin replaces him.

May 1 ▷ Tony Blair's new Labour Party wins a landslide election victory in Great Britain. He has said his first three priorities are "Education, education, education."

August 31 ▷ Diana, Princess of Wales, and her friend Dodi Fayed are killed in a car crash in Paris.

September 5 ▷ Mother Teresa, founder of the Missionaries of Charity, dies in Calcutta.

September 20 ▷ Smog covers Indonesia and Malaysia after fires started in order to clear forest rage out of control in Borneo and Sumatra.

1998

January ▷ Matt Drudge, who posts unverified news and gossip on the Internet, publishes details of President Clinton's affair with Monica Lewinsky.

April 16 ▷ Pol Pot, leader of the Khmer Rouge, who ruled Cambodia with terror from 1975 to 1979, dies. He was never brought to justice.

May 28 ▷ Pakistan explodes five nuclear devices in retaliation for nuclear tests carried out by India.

October 18 ▷ Former dictator General Pinochet is arrested in a London clinic. He led a U.S.-backed military coup in Chile in 1973. Spanish judges want Great Britain to send him to trial for his part in the deaths and torture of thousands of people.

1999

February 12 ▷ The U.S. Senate acquits President Bill Clinton on two articles of impeachment—perjury before a grand jury and obstruction of justice—arising from his denials of having an affair with White House intern Monica Lewinsky.

March 24 ▷ NATO planes begin bombing Serbia. In the weeks that follow, Serbian paramilitaries intensify their attacks on ethnic Albanians in Kosovo, causing tens of thousands of refugees to flee to neighboring countries.

June 2 ▷ The ANC wins South Africa's second general election. Thabo Mbeki becomes president. Nelson Mandela—widely acclaimed as man of the century—retires.

July 16 ▷ John Kennedy Jr, along with his wife and sister-in-law, die when his private plane plunges into the Atlantic Ocean off the coast of Massachusetts.

August 17 ▷ A major earthquake strikes Turkey, killing around 15,000.

Glossary

aborigines

The original inhabitants of Australia, who were there when the Europeans arrived in the 1700s.

African National Congress (ANC)

A civil rights organization founded in 1912. Declared illegal by the South African government, which imprisoned its leaders or forced them into exile, the ANC continued to lead the struggle against apartheid. The ban on the party was lifted in 1990, and it won the general elections held in 1994 and 1999.

AIDS

Acquired Immune Deficiency Syndrome, a fatal disease that first became known in the early '80s.

blockbuster

Word describing a movie made on a large-scale budget, often with extravagant locations and a large cast, which attracts big audiences and makes big profits.

BSE

Bovine spongiform encephalopathy. Disease that attacks the brains of cows, causing them to lose coordination of movement and then to die.

BST

Bovine somatotrophine. A synthetic hormone injected into cows to boost the quantity of milk they produce.

colonized

Settled and run by people from another country, for their profit and benefit. In the 18th and 19th centuries, some European countries established empires made up of colonies all around the world. Some of these broke free through revolutionary war and some achieved independence through political agitation. Some remained as colonies into the 1990s (for instance, Hong Kong).

El Niño

Spanish name, meaning "the child," given to warming in the Pacific Ocean that occurs in certain years, affecting the world's climate in dramatic ways.

fundamentalist

Committed to a particular faith in an extreme or rigid way; especially allowing only a literal interpretation of religious texts and no modernization of doctrine or forms of worship.

hereditary peer

Member of the British aristocracy, entitled to sit in the House of Lords (the upper chamber of parliament) as the first-born son, or otherwise heir, of a previously designated "noble" family.

hyped

Promoted excessively.

Inuit

Once known as Eskimos, the Inuit are an ancient people living in Canada, Greenland, and Alaska, whose traditional way of life revolved around hunting and fishing.

genetically modified

Techniques that enable scientists to alter the genetic material in a plant or animal, through manipulating cells in a laboratory and then introducing the cells back into the plant or animal. Some people are afraid this may bring harmful, and as yet unforeseen, consequences both to nature and to humans.

Good Friday Agreement

Agreement signed in 1998, which provided for the setting up of a power-sharing executive in Northern Ireland, including Sinn Fein as well as Social Democrat and Unionist leaders. Cross-border authorities, overseen by the British and Irish governments, would cover certain areas of policy. Over time, paramilitary organizations must give up their weapons, and prisoners convicted of terrorist offenses will be released.

landless peasants

Subsistence farmers whose land has been taken over by private individuals, companies, or government agencies, often for deforestation or mining.

millennium

A period of 1,000 years

NATO

North Atlantic Treaty Organization. Military alliance involving the United States, Great Britain and various European nations, set up to guarantee post-World War II stability in western Europe.

Nobel Prize

A highly prestigious prize awarded each year in Sweden for achievement on a world scale in the fields of Literature, Science, and Peace.

no-fly zone

Area over which aircraft of a particular country are not allowed to fly. In the 1990s, no-fly zones were created in Iraq, to prevent Saddam Hussein's planes from attacking Kurdish regions, and in Bosnia, to stop Serb air attacks. The zones were enforced by United Nations forces.

Palestine Liberation Organization (PLO)

The PLO was set up to represent Palestinian Arabs forced from their land when the Jewish state of Israel was established in 1948.

patented

New inventions are officially registered, and given a patent, to keep them from being copied or stolen and to protect the commercial interest of the inventor. Others wishing to use the new invention must have the permission of the patent owner.

prequel

George Lucas subtitled his 1977 movie *Star Wars* as episode 4 in the story of a galaxy far, far away. Two sequels made a trilogy. In 1999, his new film telling the story leading up to episode 4 was called a prequel. It was called *The Phantom Menace*.

Special Economic Zones

Areas of modern China where foreign investment and free enterprise are allowed. Internal borders separate these from the rest of China.

USSR

Union of Soviet Socialist Republics, a communist country founded out of the old Russian empire after the Bolshevik revolution of 1917.

New Words in the 1990s

New words or terms coined in the 1990s help give an idea of what was going on in the decade.

Many new words were concerned with computers. The **Internet** became a valuable source of information, and since so much new technology came from California, the word used to describe the activity of browsing through all this information came from the West Coast too. But you didn't need a beach or breakers to **surf the net**.

Once **online**, you could send and receive messages via **e-mail**, or be involved in **computer conferencing**. A fast-growing part of the Internet was the **World Wide Web** (**www**), on which people created **web sites** from which others could **download** information. **Search engines** were given unpretentious names such as Dogpile, Metacrawler, and Yahoo.

No matter who you were, you should never leave young children **home alone**. You should try to be **politically correct** (**pc**) in what you said and did, especially as regards racism and sexism. But perhaps **girl power** had gone too far, with the way girls were outperforming boys in exams. But women still said, when it came to promotion at work, that they seemed to hit an invisible barrier of prejudice that stopped them from going further – a kind of **glass ceiling**.

Index